Strategies for Time Management

Strategies for Time Management

Table Of Contents

Forward

Chapter 1:
Leadership Calls For Time Management

Chapter 2:
What Causes Poor Time Management

Chapter 3:
Procrastination

Chapter 4:
Realizing Your Present Productivity

Chapter 5:
How To Prevent Disasters

Chapter 6:
Learn To Delegate

Chapter 7:
Time Management Techniques

Chapter 8:
Avoid Interruptions

Wrapping Up

Foreword

Work at home entrepreneurs seek ways to avoid the conventional dynamics of working. They're looking for creative, more outlined ways to make a living online.

Whether that business is providing a product, a service or both, there's a quest to offer something that's
1.) Valuable and offers buyers what they wish
2.) Desired by the general population and
3.) Comparatively easy to sell and market

There's a search for freedom and a lucrative revenue that in a lot of cases may only be satisfied by the solace of working from the comforts of home. This is why the thought of working from home has gotten so popular and has many would-be business owners questing after their aspirations of owning their own businesses that they may begin, run and manage all from the comforts of their home.

A lot of entrepreneurs are in search of (and several have discovered) the perfect net business, with the perfect product or service.
They've discovered that they're able to enjoy the best of all worlds by living the entrepreneur's dream. Finding that dream for them is occasionally the first step in developing a life that's free from constraints, limits and lots of "no's". For them, life is good! But time management is essential.

Time Management Strategies For The Knowledge Worker

Understanding The Evolution Of Time Management Strategies And Prioritizing What Works In The 21st Century.

Chapter 1:
Leadership Calls For Time Management

Synopsis

A good time manager is likewise thought to be a great leader. How come? Because they take the essential steps toward accomplishing goals for their business. They look around and discover things and areas that need fine-tuning and apply principles toward making them work.

A great time manager likewise knows how to lead and motivate other people in discovering originative ways to make better use of their time. They lead by example and are free with their assistance and info.

As leaders, they perpetually share ways, tips and techniques on becoming a better manager of time, states of affairs and conditions.

Leadership

Running business online calls for the entrepreneur to be an effective manager of their time, enabling them to grapple several projects or businesses at one time, and, being able to manage them all in an efficient fashion.

The net entrepreneur can't enjoy any of their business success if they're dropping off customers, running out of time - not being able to bill their customers for that time, or unable to complete their projects.

Being able to successfully handle projects is among the key indicators of a home business enterpriser who manages their time well. Do they manage by crises or by intent? Is it part of their goal to go either slowly or quickly in project management, aiming toward a wanted result?

The affect that this may have on the work from home entrepreneur impacts any potential succeeding business and may likewise taint their net reputation. All of this is tied into suitable and effective time management! Is there an answer for this hurdle?

Time = Management

Managing time effectively is maybe the number 1 goal of most every work at home enterpriser on their quest for success. Without having effective time management, their net businesses suffer despairingly.

Making originative utilization of their time is the goal of most every work at home enterpriser who wishes to be successful in their home businesses. Effective time management will let the work at home entrepreneur be able to achieve more with their time and have fulfilled buyers and a well-fixed business.

Effective time management calls for a determined range of skills, strategies and tools and helps the net entrepreneur use them in order to achieve particular tasks, projects and goals. Without the strategic utilization of their time, they're basically wasting their time and unable to complete crucial business goals.

It's really crucial for the net entrepreneur to effectively manage time in their home business for a lot of reasons:

➢ They may complete projects in a timely manner

If they're able to be effective in finishing projects, they may take on more work; more employees and better fulfill their client loads by efficiently meeting deadlines.

➢ They're better able to create quality work

More quality work results when there's more time and more attention to particulars given to the work. Quality work may only be a result of careful tending and thoroughness to detail.

➢ They may secure more work as they're able to meet deadlines

As a work at home enterpriser, meeting deadlines for your customers is like guaranteed work! Virtually everything on the Net is time-sensitive so when you're able to meet deadlines, you show that you're responsible and committed to the task at hand.

➤ R.O.I.

There's a substantial return on investment with attention to particulars in the home business of the entrepreneur once they may effectively handle their time. If they may get more done in the course of a span of time, they lessen the amount of time to get the job accomplished, but are still able to make the same, if not more cash. The return on their investment (planning time) is fantastic!

➤ Gratification

There's an overall feeling of gratification and achievement when the online entrepreneur completes a task. The feeling of completion acts as a motivator and provides him or her creative spark they require to either approach a fresh customer or stir up more business with old customers.

These factors are commonly motivators for the work at home enterpriser to handle their time well and discover originative ways to work more efficiently. It's commonly the little details of running a business (like managing time) that help the entrepreneur make good on his business matters.

All the same, there are not always good times or simple times when all goes well with the entrepreneur who attempts to get a lot of things done in the course of their business relations. When they're responsible for each phase of their business, there's always the potential of failure or frustration for lack of planning or organizing.

What occurs when time management doesn't work well or produce the wanted results?

Are all net entrepreneurs challenged on the subject of time management?

There are times that the work from home enterpriser discovers that their systems and procedures aren't working. They discover that regardless what they do, they can't remain focused and finish the tasks or goals that they have. They discover that they're basically poorly managing their time and unable to accomplish neither small nor big goals.

What may be the perpetrator? Poor management of time.

Chapter 2:

What Causes Poor Time Management

Synopsis

Second-rate time management - - does the net entrepreneur ever believe that he has poor time management? Or, does he automatically believe that he's managing his time efficiently and effectively merely because he's a business owner?

Either way, he has to cautiously guard against wasting time or not maximizing the full utilization of the flexible time that work at home entrepreneurs have. Without a self-asserting effort, he may be doomed for incompleteness or merely business failure.

Frequently, procrastination is the primary perpetrator of poor time management, but is frequently not taken as seriously as of the perceived "creativity" in waiting. Put differently, net entrepreneurs frequently have trepidation about moving too fast on business projects or making decisions too rapidly.

As noble as this might sound, it may often have the opposite effect and cause the work from home individual to move too slowly, move too fast or do nothing at all. Good time management may help.

What Harms Time Management

Failing to plan in any home business isn't different from failing to plan in any other sort of business. There must be a business model formulated, a marketing strategy followed out and a plan of action to accomplish goals for the business. This all ties into the ability to design, effectively handle time and resources and discovering what works for the business.

Planning daily might seem like a lot of work to do but in actual truth when it becomes a habit, it gets to be second nature. Studies show that it takes an average of twenty-one times for something to get to be a habit. When something does get to be a habit, it's much simpler to maintain than if it's new or from the beginning.

Home entrepreneurs have total flexibility and convenience in their occupations. There's no one standing over them, ordering their day, telling them what to accomplish, when to accomplish it, how to accomplish it, and so forth. With all of this freedom, an undisciplined individual won't understand how to effectively manage their time or when to say no to particular projects or fresh business.

For a lot of entrepreneurs, they put off their work duties or obligations for wide-ranging reasons. Doing this may cause unbelievable tension for the entrepreneur and cause them to handle or work in a crises mode.

Working in that way may produce additional issues that may become hard to solve or manage. There are errors made, uncompleted projects, missed goals, second-rate work quality and even second-rate business results.

Chapter 3:
Procrastination

Synopsis

What are a few of the major reasons how come home entrepreneurs dilly-dally?

Why is it that they put off arriving at decisions, beginning fresh projects, pursuing fresh business or even completing big projects that have impact on more business for them?

Let's take a few reasons how come:

Dilly-Dally

- The net entrepreneur has second-rate work habits

The work at home enterpriser who has second-rate work habits is commonly slow starting at everything. They're habitual procrastinators and take very long periods of time to finish projects or get anything accomplished.

- What may result from this sort of net business activity?

Defeat and loss in business and sales. If they miss a deadline or they fail to communicate with their buyers or clients that may result in a loss of business and a damaging viewpoint of their net reputation. This isn't good for any would-be net and web entrepreneur.

Very frequently, they likewise procrastinate on everything else in their lives, including personal regions, and are forever attempting to "catch up". This stimulates high tension levels and low production levels.

The net entrepreneur who has second-rate work habits is likewise under the impression that they execute better under pressure. Not truthful.

They think that they may do their best work if they're forced to work quicker, activating their creativity. Not truthful. What all of this does is merely place them further behind in their work and cause more tension. Period.

- They've continual feelings of being overpowered

The net entrepreneur who's challenged in the area of effective time management frequently feels like they never have anything achieved. They frequently don't do anything at all in reaction to either being proactive in their work or in completing tasks.

The overpowering feeling may also lead to anxiety and the propensity to make huge, expensive errors in their work. It's generally known that when you're tired or overwhelmed, the capacity and possibility of making errors step-ups exponentially. Naturally, this adds even more to the feeling of being overmastered and feeling under-accomplished.

There's likewise a feeling of uselessness in business projects with enterprisers who procrastinate. They feel like it might be easier to do nothing at all because of the sheer size of what their undertaking is. This once again is cyclic and may induce a spiral effect in the business. Because one thing doesn't get accomplished, it causes a different thing to not get accomplished and the process may continue and may cause even more issues.

- They feel that they must be "perfect"

This is quite potentially among the most common but most damaging personality traits that a work from home enterpriser has. To a fault, they feel that they must be perfect, avoid all errors at all costs, get things correct the first time and be able to totally and pointedly satisfy the customer's every impulse and need. It isn't only unrealistic to believe this, but it's likewise damaging and unfair for the entrepreneur to expect if of himself.

Expecting perfectionism is a false belief of the net entrepreneur. There's no way that they may be perfect, and they place undue tension on themselves by doing so.

They wish to finish projects, meet deadlines, achieve goals and do them all at record speed! But what holds them back is frequently merely getting moving.

They might view their business projects as taxing and shun them as insignificant. This frequently makes them feel better as they're able to convince themselves that if they're not crucial, then it might be just as insignificant to their clients or buyers. The entrepreneur will commonly put off completion till the project meets their standards for perfection.

Although this percept is only appreciated by the enterpriser, these standards are frequently not recognized by their customers. This naturally reinforces the fact that it's a time waster and they've worked unprofitably towards an unnecessary end.

> The entrepreneur is blasé

Blasé? Do work at home enterprisers truly get bored? Certainly they do! But not in the sense where tedium is frequently utilized.

They get blasé with no creativity or change in their work. Although they might perhaps love what they do, they discover that doing the same thing day in day out becomes humdrum and non-challenging for them. Therefore, their boredom sets in and they lose interest in the projects that they're working on.

A lot of times, the work at home individual would merely rather be doing something else besides working. Does that mean they're lazy? Scarcely! They frequently just don't understand where to begin or how to manage their business projects or how to jumpstart something in their business to get their interests.

They might seek other originative outlets that are not business related, like engaging on social sites or community discussion boards rather than really working. Everyday tasks like paperwork or net jobs may take precedence over really doing work.

The entrepreneur will merely keep putting tasks off, wishing they'd either magically become shorter or disappear. Their tension level may increase, knowing that this undertaking is bound to not happen, and may make their jobs harder to achieve and goals harder to realize.

What are the results of these snares? Do you practice effective time management?

Chapter 4:

Realizing Your Present Productivity

Synopsis

Here are a few matters to bear in mind that may drastically affect your productivity rate when it comes to your business:

What's Happening Now

> ➤ Beginning your day with no action plan

If you begin your day with no action plan, you're damned from the start! You start off late and feel overpowered from the beginning. You then spend your day in a defensive and crisis mood.

You might likewise find yourself hurriedly and arbitrarily responding to other people's issues and events and place them higher up than your own issues.

> ➤ No equilibrium

There are 7 key areas in our lives where we have to practice equilibrium in order to feel and have success:

- Wellness - how your body feels and how it reacts to external stimulants
- Loved ones - quality time and responsibilities with loved ones
- Financial - amount of fiscal burdens and revenue obligations
- Intellectual - how exterior stimulants affect your life
- Social - how you interact with other people
- Professional - the procedures that you utilize to advance your career
- Spiritual - your relationship with the higher power and other people

Each of these areas calls for our daily time for completeness, although they might not all get equal time every day. It's not so crucial to spend significant time in every area, but it's crucial to spend a little time in every area.

In the long haul, our lives will be balanced and harmonious if we spend a sufficient amount and quality of time in every area. All the same, if we disregard any one of these areas, we may quickly sabotage our success.

For example, if we don't take care of our wellness, our loved ones and social life suffer. Likewise, if we're out of balance in our monetary resources, we can't adequately center on our professional goals, career dreams and additional crucial areas of focus.

> Cluttered up workspace

A cluttered up workspace may produce a cluttered up work brain.

Issues result when you can't find crucial business documents or locate info for your customers. These things induce mayhem, wreak bedlam and confusion, but may likewise lead to lost revenue and delayed billing.

Studies have been conducted, proving that an individual who works with a cluttered up desk spends about one to two hours a day searching for things or being distracted by them. This may add up significantly in hours squandered per week.

> Poor rest

The perpetrator of poor rest is the blame for a lot of net entrepreneurs not meeting goals or seeing results in their businesses. Not enough sleep may lead to poorly made decisions or irrational selections as they relate to crucial business functions.

Studies have evidenced that nearly 75% of net enterprisers are sleep-deprived, and that their businesses are inadvertently impacted. Being tired isn't good or productive for the work at home individual.

If the deficiency of sleep doesn't negatively impact the entrepreneur, the caliber of their sleep will. This implies that when they do get to rest, it's commonly fitful, restless sleep because of fundamental stress and other debilitating components.

Stress-filled days are hazardous to the net entrepreneur and may eventually become detrimental. The key is to acquire enough rest and proper sleep to experience less tension and become more productive.

> Not taking breaks

Taking decent breaks and frequent breaks is a big failure of the net entrepreneur. Because they're not on a routine or rigid schedule as in a corporate scene, they feel that they shouldn't have to or can't consider breaks. They might likewise feel that doing so is a waste of time. Not truthful. Taking sufficient breaks is vital to daily successes.

A lot of times, the net entrepreneur likewise neglects to take sufficient breaks as they feel as though they may produce better results.

They feel that if they work straight through, that they may get more accomplished and be more productive. This doesn't produce more results or even better work time.

If the body is exhausted, reaction and creativity are gravely hampered and may cause the quality of the entrepreneur's work to suffer.

Chapter 5:

How To Prevent Disasters

Synopsis

Have a look at the ways you can prevent disasters from happening.

Do It Right

➢ Produce schemes that work

To make better utilization of your time in your home business, produce schemes that flow and work well inside your work space. Systematize and organize stuff so that there's a procedure that leads one step to work with the next step and so forth and so on. Don't begin over every time you have to produce something.

➢ Produce schemes to address repetitive jobs

This would include any paper and/or digital technology that you'd utilize to get the job done in your business. Forever have enough supplies available that you are able to readily get at.

Utilize a calendar, digital or paper, to keep track of appointments. You are able to see what, wear and when you have to do what every day, at-a-glance. This may help you successfully plan your day for optimum results.

Forever work with a clean desk, with papers filed and organized and forever have the most frequently utilized items for your business in your immediate grasp.

➢ Plan enough rest periods

Sleep authorities recommend for the normal, healthy grownup to get at least eight hours of sleep a night. This helps them to function decently and be really productive, yet a poll by the National Sleep Foundation's 2000 Sleep in America omnibus poll discovered that, on the average, grownups sleep just under seven hours during the work week.

As an enterpriser, you ought to schedule a sufficient amount of rest for optimal productivity. The amount is different for each of us and you ought to let your body see what circumstances it works best under.

Some require 8 hours, some more, others less. Your body recognizes the answer.

> Formulate Your communicating skills

Your ability to aptly and confidently communicate what you understand both orally and in writing is extremely crucial to your business' success. Make it an in progress commitment to continue to better your speaking and writing skills. You'll save time and have a more successful vocation.

Chapter 6:
Learn To Delegate

Synopsis

Delegation is all-important to time management. The ability to efficiently delegate allows you as a net entrepreneur the freedom and flexibleness to work on additional projects.

Know When To Turn It Over

To optimize your time, make certain to arrange a realistic and reachable deadline for any delegated work that you dispense. Make certain that the delegation is fair and balanced and is workable for the individual to whom you assigned to. Always be particular about what you want done when you delegate work so as to prevent any confusion and to make certain that you accomplish the desired outcomes necessary.

When delegating, be really clear-cut about the purpose of the work that you're delegating and what sort of outcomes you anticipate. Beware of delegating without directions, as it may cause bedlam, disarray and second-rate work quality. If you lack the time to give the individual complete and explicit directions, you might wish to give the work to an individual who may manage with little interaction from you. This will keep you from micro managing and free you up to be more productive.

Always let the individual to whom you delegated be originative in their work. Merely seek and expect quality outcomes without dictating step-by-step on how the project is to be executed. This neutralizes your whole purpose of delegating and may likewise cause undue tension.

Devise a scheme to report back to you to get feedback on the individual's progress. This keeps you from being perpetually disrupted during the day. Keep a list of vital dates so that you acquire the feedback on a regular basis. Make sure to likewise keep a log of all your delegated projects and update the log as you acquire feedback.

Chapter 7:
Time Management Techniques

Synopsis

Utilize these techniques to manage your time better.

Manage It Better

- Preparation

Take time to set aside at least 10 minutes every evening to schedule the following day. You ought to normally schedule about 60-70% of your time to allow for disruptions and emergencies. Draw from your list of things that are high priority and arrange blocks of time where you work at a particular area of your business.

- Organize

Take the time to organize your office by class. Do this by putting all of your pertinent files and info that corresponds together in one place. Put all of your financial paperwork together. Put all of your financial-related matters together. This will help you center on one project at a time and be a welcomed time-saver. Orchestrate your office in addition to orchestrating your time. Utilization lists to keep yourself centered and on track. Being organized is a continual procedure. Spending a couple of hours organizing yourself now will save you 100s of hours in the time to come.

- File Systems

A great filing and paperwork system will let you be highly productive. Set your files to reflect the following things:

- To accomplish

Naturally, this would hold everything that you aim to accomplish or have accomplished on a periodic basis, whether that's every day, every week, every quarter or every month. Succinct to accomplish lists are vital to the success of the home business person. You ought to and may likewise file away any old to accomplish lists after having finished them. This will give you archived data and referencing in case you have to go back and seek client or project info.

> To study

There is not adequate time in the entrepreneur's day to study all of the e-mails, postal mail material, magazines, e-books and catalogs that come across his desk or PC. When you've info that's coming from a lot of sources both online and offline, you have to be certain to keep them organized for future reference. File away this material for future reviewing and studying when more time is permissible.

Keep a tickler file online and offline so that you are able to easily access them both at will. Particularly in cases of net filing, you are able to do several matters to better manage your time.

1.) Sort your mail into a digital folder with a label. Makes it simpler to find for future access.

2.) Upload it to your e-mail inbox or e-mail provider.

3.) Transfer the folder to your PDA or additional technological devices

4.) Later or if time permits, view the correspondence and either a.) Erase it or b.) to act on it

> Thoughts

Utilize the thoughts folder to hold your originative thoughts and any future thoughts you have for the business. This may likewise be a part of your goals and goal setting, but ought to definitely hold creative thinking thoughts and sparks. You are able to likewise utilize this folder to hold additional ideas or marketing strategies that you chance upon. This is to set the stage to spark more thoughts inside you when you review the folder. This folder has the potential to grow significantly as a big part of any home business is promoting, promoting, promoting.

> Resolutions

This folder will bear resolutions to either correspondence that you've sent to likely or present customers or answers that you're providing for yourself. Don't know how much you charged for that final project you did for X Customer? Look in the resolutions folder. What about the quote that you gave the net phone directory company after they asked about your telecommerce services…it may very well be in the resolutions folder. Resolutions may be in response to questions that you've sent out or have received into your office.

> References

The reference folder is vital to your business and helps enormously with marketing efforts. You ought to have correspondence that is referrals for preceding jobs and letters of recommendations in that folder. The reference folder ought to (and may) likewise hold references that you require for other types of projects where another individual is needed. Put differently, if you are a content author but have to find a web designer, look in your reference folder and see who recommends whom as that. This may be a priceless piece of time management and organizational tool for your business. Maximize its utilization by notating and documenting pertinent and relevant info that's highly targeted to particular niche areas.

- Copies

Everything that happens upon your desk ought to be copied in some manner. That includes purchase receipts, contracts, bills, tax info, client work orders and any and everything that pertains to your business. In order to lessen the amount of clutter that this may cause, digitally copy everything and store it on your PC or on a back-up disk. Very simply, scan documents into your PC and save it to a specified area. This makes it much simpler to recall it when you require it.

- File

Pretty self-explanatory, this tickler file is for everything that has to be filed away. Develop a scheme that's simple to remember and takes the guessing out of "where may it be?" This system will let you find the info that you want when you want it, keeping it out of your way and off of your desk.

- PC

Learn to utilize your computer effectively and efficiently. Discover ways to take full advantage of it and maximize its utilization for your business. Invest in courses or at least buy how-to books for every program in your system. Your PC may make your days more productive and streamlined toward effective time management if it's properly utilized. Learning it in its totality and the numerous features that it has will help you make better utilization of your time.

- Creative thinking

Creative thinking is the spark and backbone of any successful net business. Without it, ideas can't take form and businesses can't be formed. A mind that's relaxed, stress-free and happy is more conducive to sparks and bouts of creative thinking and has more time to center fully on attaining good business. Spend originative time thinking, reading and exploring ways and thoughts that may improve your business. Little bits of time on a day-to-day basis may help and result in effective techniques.

- Preparation

Daily preparation the night before work the next day helps to produce a synchronized system to help you in your business. A great plan can't be arbitrarily fudged together but has to be meticulously designed. Without a plan of action in place before beginning your day, you run the risk of getting out of focus and distracted. A plan of action, developed the night before is a blueprint for success for the following day. You understand what your next steps are and what your goals for the days ought to be. You work diligently toward that effort, recognizing that once you're done, goals (large or small) are achieved and you are able to move on to the next project for your business.

- Delineating projects

Making an outline of projects will help the work at home person make more beneficial use of their days and maximize utilization of their time. In order to see a more generative day, it's great to begin with an outline and work from it. Firstly, list where you want the end result of the project to be. From there, work backward and formulate the steps that it will take to get there. After that, conclude the outline with the opening move of the project and the brainstorming idea(s) that were used to spark the project from the outset. Once you work this way, you're basically reducing big projects to smaller, manageable sorts to see results. Work slower, more methodically and cautiously to avoid making errors.

> Plan around disruptions

Disruptions tend to happen in identifiable patterns with most of them occurring early in the day versus later in the day. Disruptions are never handy nor do they "choose" a time to occur. Plan for bigger projects for later in the day and later in the week when there tends to be fewer disruptions.

> Allot deadlines

Deadlines move individuals to action and acquire quick results. Without deadlines, matters simply get accomplished when they get accomplished with no haste behind them. Make a deadline and you'll be moved to action.

Chapter 8:
Avoid Interruptions

Synopsis

Many of the disruptions we deal as net entrepreneurs may be eliminated with a little focus and determination. One way to acquire better control is to utilize a log to record apiece instance of interruptions. To do this, record the accompanying data into 6 columns:

Keep Track

1. Date

Record the date of the disruption. Keep a log of this just as you would customer and client interactions and any additional type of communication that you'd deem crucial. This will help you when you refer back to it for additional info.

2. Time

A lot of times, your days are busier than others just as particular times of the day are busier than others. It might not be feasible for you to take particular calls at particular times of the day as opposed to other times of the day. Record the time that you take the disruption call, so as to note any developing patterns, schemes, and so forth.

You might likewise wish to record the time in any digital products that you might have which will make simpler for future referencing and notating. Pay especial attention to patterns developing during a set time of day, week, and so forth.

3. Who

If it's another call from grandmother, log it. If it's another call from the phone marketers, notate that too. Recognize and log who's calling you and disturbing your work day.

Are there any repeat wrongdoers? You might wish to take note of this and adapt your schedule accordingly in order to prevent them.

4. What

Note what sort of info the call is about. Is it business related at all or simply plain prattle? This may be and typically is where the bulk of the time wasters are discovered. During business hours is the time to talk over...business!!

Work at home enterprisers are frequently the unfortunate victims of assuming that they're not working because they're at home. Disruption calls will occasionally be silly calls like recipe requests, calls to "vent" or unfounded gossip. Understand and record what the conversation was about.

5. Duration

How long are the calls lasting? A couple of minutes here and there might not hurt, but may add up quickly! Be strong yet gentle when you're trying to end your interruption calls that are fruitless for your business.

6. Rating

Rate the call based on the previous 6 factors along with a grading scale similar to this:

A=essential
B=significant
C=little value
D=no value

Plan to record this info for about a week to get a precise measure of what is truly occurring. If it was worth your while, rate either high or low based on your tastes. This will help you to better ascertain where your time goes and how it's being used.

After you've amassed this data for a week, go back and total up all of the A's, B's, C's, and D's to see where you have to correct things. Most individuals find that more than 50% of their disruptions were C's and D's and were matters that weren't worth the time spent.

After this, examine each C and D disruption and see how they may have been avoided. Take proactive steps to see to it that it won't repeat itself in the future. Do this particularly for the repetitive disruptions.

A lot of times, individuals will come to you for information that they may have located themselves.

To remedy this, show this individual how to find the info themselves or they'll continue to disrupt you to get it. It's easier for them this way, but more difficult for you and your available time. Show them how to get what they require on their own.

Wrapping Up

Make things as easy as possible. This means streamlining procedures and making things work easier. For example, if you take credit cards in your business, make that more available than having to deal with checks that have to be carried to the bank, cashed and/or deposited. If there are steps to a procedure that may be eliminated, do that and watch your productivity zoom.

The more you simplify, the simpler it will be for your business to run. Things and procedures run smoother with fewer steps and decrease the possibilities of mistakes.

Simplification is an excellent tool for finding more time.

As well, use leveraging. The concept of leveraging refers to getting and utilizing multiple resources of things out of materials you've already created. Although it may take a particular amount of skill and creativity to do this well, in the long haul it may pay off double times in value.

When you get into the habit of leveraging, you may significantly multiply your returns from a one-time investment of your work. In producing new materials for your business, continually ask yourself, "How may I utilize this again?"

www.ingramcontent.com/pod-product-compliance
Lightning Source LLC
LaVergne TN
LVHW020501080526
838202LV00057B/6079